Psst...Rose Discovered a Secret

Written and Illustrated by

Ali Goebel

Published by Heritage Publishing.US.

www.heritagepublishingus.com

This book was inspired by Ruby Reinhardt

(March 23, 1914—January 10, 2017)

who wrote a story about her adored granddaughter ,

Rose Reinhardt

Have you ever heard of a little town called Nelson? In Nelson, Wisconsin there is a magical farm where only children can see and feel its magic.

Children know how to look and see with their hearts—as a young girl, named Rose, knew very well.

Rose lived and played on this magical farm with her two brothers Paul and Randy.

She loved being surrounded by all the hills, tall trees, and colorful wildflowers.

What Rose loved most were the unusual creatures that she would often catch glimpses of.

When Rose looked patiently with her heart
she found a dragon. Dragons brought gifts of
courage and the ability to fly to humans.

Often, Rose would see a fairy flitting through the wildflowers. Fairies helped make the trees and flowers grow. She felt there must be a lot of fairies living on her farm because there were sooooo many beautiful things growing there.

Sometimes, Rose even spotted a unicorn or two. She believed unicorns could make dreams come true.

Winding through this magical place, was a lively dancing creek. Many creatures that Rose knew and loved gathered there to drink the fresh rambling water.

One summer day, Rose ran as fast as she could down the hill to join her brothers playing in the creek. Suddenly, she realized she was still wearing her new pretty shoes. They were shiny black on the outside and brilliant blue on the inside. Because she didn't want to get them wet or dirty, she took them off, and with a little love pat she placed them at the edge of the creek.

The three children were gathering colorful pebbles and stones from the creek's floor, when Rose suddenly yelled, "Oh no! NO! NO! Paul, Randy! Come help me! One of my new shoes is gone."

Then Rose spotted her new shoe bobbing happily down–stream away from them into deeper water. Not even the boys could go that far to retrieve her little shoe…that was shiny black on the outside and brilliant blue on the inside.

Rose and her brothers sat down on the creek's bank.
Rose felt very sad. Paul and Randy were sad for Rose.

Rose picked up her lonely shoe and tearfully went to find her mother. Not wanting her little girl to be sad, her mother tried to console Rose by saying, "Just think, your little shoe is probably having lots of fun while traveling to faraway places."

Rose watched curiously as her mother opened a large map of the United States. "Our little farm is here," said Mother— pointing to a squiggly line on the map. "Our creek joins the Chippewa River, which meets the big Mississippi River."

The Mississippi River flows through ten states until it pours into the Gulf of Mexico, and then into the great Atlantic Ocean. It became obvious to Rose that her new little shoe, shiny black on the outside and brilliant blue on the inside, would be traveling a great distance.

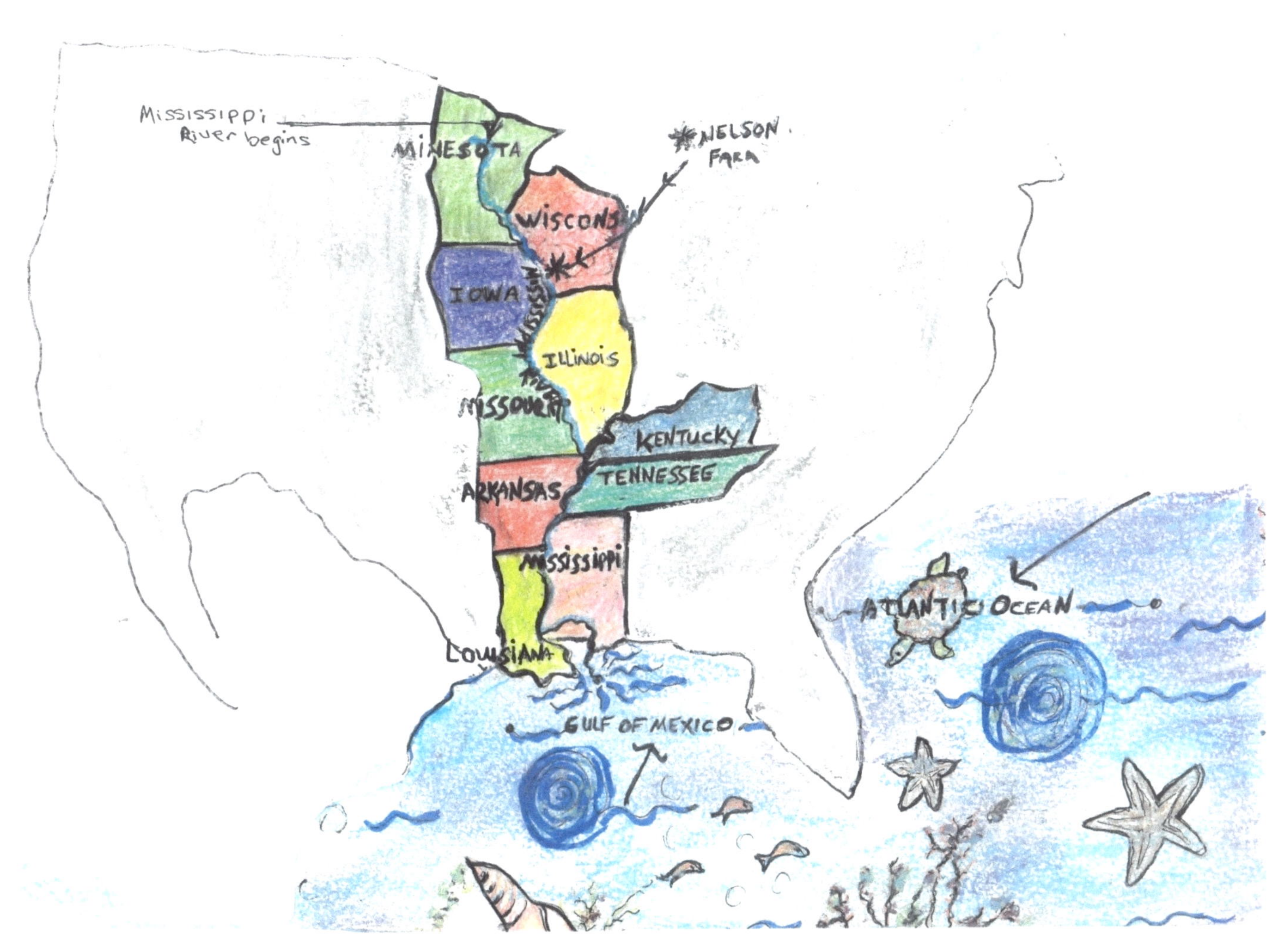

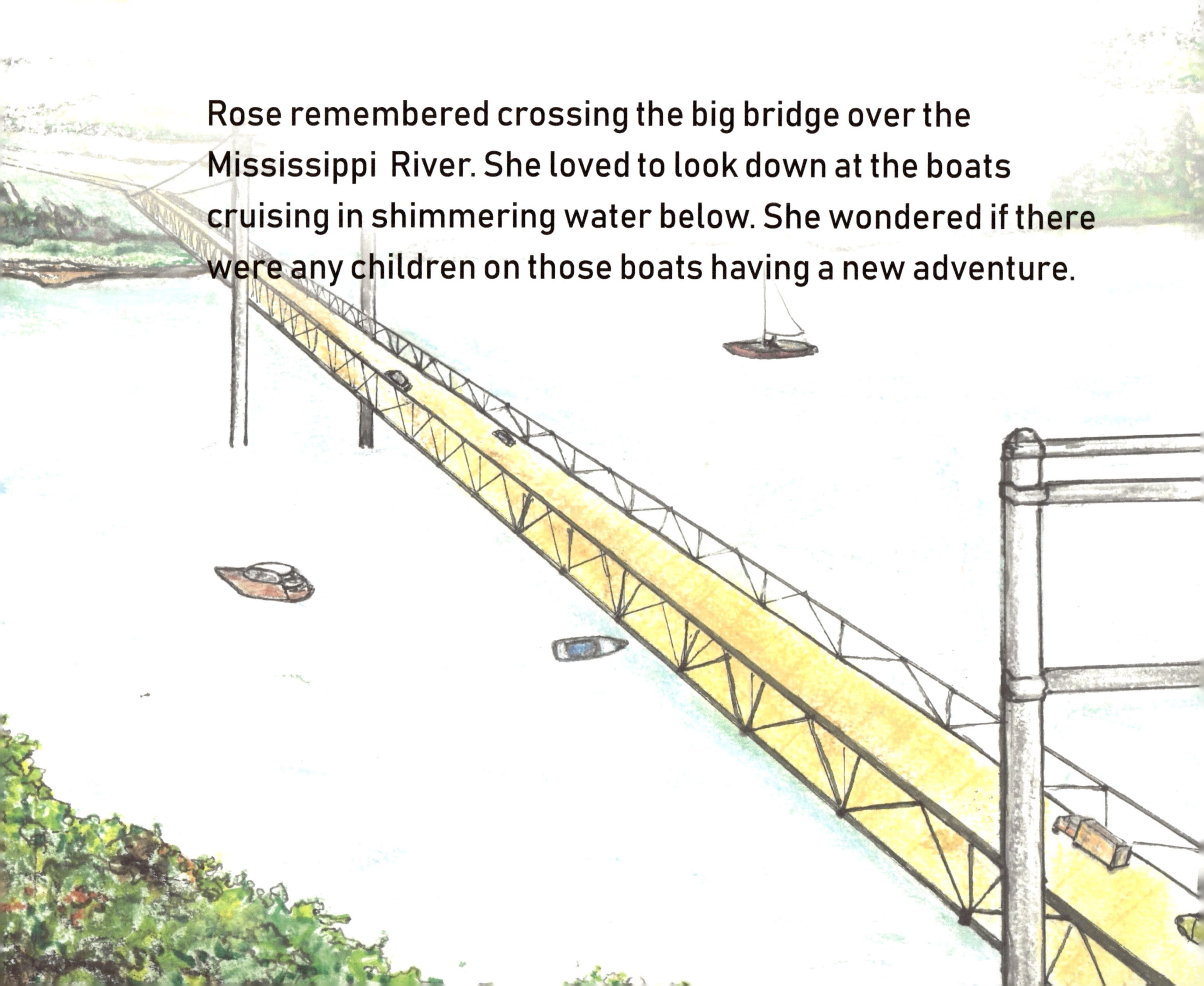

Rose remembered crossing the big bridge over the Mississippi River. She loved to look down at the boats cruising in shimmering water below. She wondered if there were any children on those boats having a new adventure.

Rose and her mother decided to plan a trip to search for Rose's new shoe—that was shiny black on the outside and brilliant blue on the inside. Rose knew that the chances of finding her little shoe were very slim indeed.

She began to imagine the big world out there—far away from her safe home on the magical farm in Nelson, Wisconsin.

After several days of searching, Rose's mother said, " I think by now your new little shoe has made its way to the great Atlantic Ocean. Now, we have to say goodbye, and wish your shoe a happy journey."

Rose was a little sad again. "Will I ever go to the Atlantic Ocean?" she asked her Mother. "Oh, yes! I'm sure you will," said mother smiling. "People often fly in large airplanes across oceans, even continents."

As Rose grew up, she always kept the one little shoe among her special treasures. She often thought of her lost shoe floating down that winding creek in Wisconsin.

Because her shoe floated away from her that one summer day, she discovered a wonderful secret about herself. She realized that she also wanted to travel and experience the magic of new places around the world.

How lucky she was to have had those special new shoes
... that were shiny black on the outside and brilliant blue
on the inside.

Author's Note
Even when sad things happen to us, we
can discover something wonderful about
ourselves....
Just keep looking for the magic.

Ali Goebel has been an artist from the day she held her first crayon and paintbrush. Her art education is unconventional. She began freelancing in her teens, mentored under various artists, and studied at the local University in Evansville, Indiana. Then her life took some unexpected twists and turns, as a result the artist in her took a long nap. After 25 years, a good friend reawakened her calling by encouraging and commissioning her for a project. Her artistic momentum began to increase and manifested her first published children's book Psst...Rose Discovered a Secret which she both wrote and illustrated.

To see more of her work, visit her website AliAnnInspired.com

CPSIA information can be obtained
at www.ICGtesting.com
Printed in the USA
BVHW090216130319
542529BV00011B/42/P